Nottingham Playhouse Theatre Company

and

the Octagon Theatre, Bolton

D0067429

in association with

Theatre Writing Partnership

present

Satin 'n' Steel

by Amanda Whittington

First performance on Tuesday 1 March 2005
at Nottingham Playhouse
sponsored by

www.presence.co.uk

Friday 25 February to Saturday 12 March 2005
at Nottingham Playhouse

Nottingham Playhouse

Wednesday 6 April - Saturday 30 April 2005
at the Octagon Theatre, Bolton

octagon
Bolton

Cover photography © Robert Day

LITERATURE AND LANGUAGE DEPARTMENT
THE CHICAGO PUBLIC LIBRARY
400 SOUTH STATE STREET
CHICAGO, ILLINOIS 60605

CAST

Sara Poyzer   Teena Satin
Norman Pace   Vince Steel

CREATIVE TEAM

Amanda Whittington	Writer
Esther Richardson	Director
Helen Davies	Designer
Richard G Jones	Lighting Designer
Matthew Newbury	Assistant Lighting Designer
Stuart Briner	Musical Director/Composer
Jane Eliot-Webb	Company and Stage Manager
Anita Drabwell	Deputy Stage Manager
Kathryn Bainbridge Wilson	Assistant Stage Manager

R0414010883

Norman Pace

Vince Steel

Norman's theatre credits include: Fabian in **Twelfth Night** and Dogberry in **Much Ado About Nothing** (Open Air Shakespeare Festival, Nottingham, 2004); Amos Hart in **Chicago** (West End, 1999 & 2003); Eric in **A Slice Of Saturday Night** (UK Tour, 2002); and Bullfrog & Drake in **Honk** (UK Tour, 2001).

Television Credits include: **Casualty** (BBC); **jobs for the boys** (BBC); **Oddbods** (Talent Television for BBC1. 1998); **April Fool's Day** (Kudos Productions for LWT, 1997); **A Pinch of Snuff** (Yorkshire Television, 1993); **The Hale and Pace Show** (LWT Productions, Winner of the Golden Rose of Montreux and Press Award); and **The Management** (LWT Productions for Channel 4, 1988).

Sara Poyzer

Teena Satin

Sara's theatre credits include: **The Merchant Of Venice, Antigone** and **Poetry Or Bust** all for Northern Broadsides; **Bollywood Jane** (Leicester Haymarket); **The Fly** (Oldham Coliseum); **Up 'n' Under** (Pomengranate); **Only The Understudy, Players' Angels** (New Perspectives); **One Step Beyond** and **Wildest Dreams** (Yvonne Arnaud). Sara works extensively in radio and can currently be heard as Sylvia in **Falco: Shadows In Bronze** for BBC Radio 4. Sara's television and film credits include **Doctors, EastEnders, Dangerville, Dangerfield, Naked & Famous, Peak Practice, Playing The Field** and **Bad Hair Day**. Sara is a co-founder of Hard Graft Theatre Company for whom she has directed **Bedders & Pike, Thick As Thieves** and **Burt 'n' Joyce**.

Amanda Whittington
Writer

Amanda's most well-known play is **Be My Baby**, which has been produced by Soho Theatre, Oldham Coliseum, Hull Truck and Salisbury Playhouse. Past productions include **Bollywood Jane** (Leicester Haymarket); **The Wills's Girls** (Tobacco Factory, Bristol & Radio Four); **The Boy on the Hill**, **Last Stop Louisa's** and **Player's Angels** (New Perspectives, tour). Publications include **Be My Baby** (Nick Hern Books); **Twist & Shout**, **Runaway Girl** and **Shirley's Song** (SchoolPlay). Amanda is based in Nottingham. She was joint winner of the 2001 Dennis Potter Screenwriting Award and is currently working on a number of stage and screen projects. For more information visit **www.amandawhittington.com.**

Esther Richardson
Director

Esther is Director of Theatre Writing Partnership: a unique new writing organisation based at Nottingham Playhouse which creates and supports new productions across the theatres in the East Midlands region.

Formerly she was Assistant Dramaturg at the Royal Shakespeare Company.

Educated at Bristol University and Goldsmiths College, London, Esther's recent directing credits include: **Get Shortie** (Amanda Whittington and Andy Barrett) for Nottingham Playhouse and Royal Theatre, Northampton; **Summer Comes and Life Changes** (Andy Barrett) for New Perspectives. She has also directed work for Grid Iron, The Citizens Theatre, Glasgow, and Turtle Key Arts. Recent dramaturgy includes: **Bollywood Jane** (Amanda Whittington), **The Palace of Fear** (Philip Osment) and **The Illustrious Corpse** (Tariq Ali) for Leicester Haymarket Theatre; **Mother Courage and Her Children** (Oladipo Agboluaje) for Nottingham Playhouse.

Producing credits include: **Momentum** young writers' project (joint recipient of the Peggy Ramsay Award 2004/5); **Get Shortie** and **Season of Courage** for Nottingham Playhouse and the Royal Theatre Northampton.

Helen Davies
Designer

Helen graduated from Nottingham Trent University with a BA (Hons) in Theatre Design. In 1996 she was appointed as a Resident Designer for 6 years at the Arts and Education Centre in Nottingham, designing over 20 productions for young people's theatre, including European tours and large-scale concerts. She has also developed and facilitated workshops for young people and adults in Theatre Arts throughout Nottinghamshire.

Now working as a freelance set and costume designer her recent shows include: **The Snow Queen**, **Arabian Nights** and **The Firebird** (mac, Birmingham); **The Man Who** (Nottingham Playhouse); **Safahr** (Birmingham Royal Ballet and Creative Partnerships); **Two Minutes Silence** (a site-specific production in Shrewsbury for Focus Productions and SYT); and currently designing **A Who's Who of Flapland** (Lakeside, Nottingham).

Helen has also designed a number of shows for touring including: **The Elves and the Shoemaker** (mac Birmingham); **Bowled A Googly** (Oxford Touring Theatre Company and New Perspectives); **The Bad One** (Women and Theatre); **Zagazoo**, **Nightmaze**, **Come With Me** and **Stepping Stones** (Roundabout, Nottingham Playhouse); and **Brethren** and **3 Tales of Courage** (Eclipse Theatre).

She also enjoys continuing to support a number of Theatre Arts based projects through professional companies or independently led, that are developed for people with learning disabilities, adults and young people.

Photography by Robert Day

Richard G Jones
Lighting Designer

Richard lives in Birmingham, and his lighting designs include numerous productions in this country, abroad and in the West End.

National tours have included **Beautiful Thing**, **Wuthering Heights**, **Rasputin**, **Candide** and **Sweeney Todd**. West End work includes **The Gondoliers**, **When Pigs Fly and Female Parts** and **Sweeney Todd**. Repertory theatre work includes **Behind the Scenes at the Museum**, **A Taste of Honey**, **Piaf**, **Abandonment**, **Private Lives** and **Amadeus** for York Theatre Royal; **Carmen**, **Fiddler on the Roof**, **Irma la Douce**, and **Cabaret** for the Watermill Theatre Newbury; **The Man Who** for Nottingham Playhouse; and **The Firebird**, **The Arabian Nights**, **The Snow Queen** and **The Emperor and the Nightingale** for the mac.

Richard has recently been working on lighting designs for **Peter Pan** at Oxford Playhouse, a tour of **Midnight** for Watershed Productions and **Mack and Mabel** for The Watermill Theatre, which will tour then have a run at the Trafalgar Studios later in the year.

He has also designed for The Royal Northern College of Music, Manchester; The Norwich Playhouse; The Duchy Ballet, Cornwall; Covent Garden Linbury Studio; Culture and Congress Centre, Lucerne; The Swan Theatre, Worcester; Library Theatre, Manchester; Everyman Theatres, Liverpool and Cheltenham; Arden Theatre; the Octagon Theatre, Bolton; Birmingham REP; Oxford Playhouse and The Theatre on the Lake, Keswick. His work can be seen at **www.richardgjones.co.uk.**

Stuart Briner
Musical Director/Composer

Following success at Trinity College of Music, studying with Nona Liddell MBE FRAM and John Thomas, Stuart went on to study composition for the moving image with Professor Stephen Deutsch, film and television composer for many years at the BBC.

Stuart has composed original scores for numerous short films and animations as well as two feature films. His work includes scores for television documentaries, award-winning animations and other assorted programmes both in the United Kingdom and France.

Future projects include the technically groundbreaking short film **Out** as well as another feature length film for Anglo-French production house **Man of Straw**.

This is Stuart's third collaboration with director Esther Richardson and first work for Nottingham Playhouse.

Nottingham Playhouse
theatre company

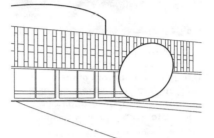

Nottingham Playhouse Theatre Company produces nine main stage productions per year, and four productions through its Theatre-In-Education company, Roundabout. During the past three years the Playhouse has toured its work to over 50 towns and cities in the UK and Europe. In 2003 it transferred its world premiere production of **Rat Pack Confidential** (another co-production with the Octagon) to The Whitehall Theatre, London and also toured **Moon on a Rainbow Shawl**, the first project of the ground-breaking Eclipse theatre initiative, nationally. In 2004 it toured a new adaptation of **Mother Courage and Her Children** as the second Eclipse project and attracted record

audiences across the country, culminating in a week at the newly restored Hackney Empire. Roundabout's production of **Mohammed** featured in the Mejnifest Celebrations to mark the accession of Slovenia into the European Community in May 2004. In 2005 it transfers its highly successful production of **The Railway Children** to The Peacock theatre in London for a three week run.

Nottingham Playhouse has a commitment to commissioning new work and has staged five world premieres on its main stage in the past year. During 2003-2004 it has been nominated for 10 theatre awards, winning the City Life award for Best Production for **Rat Pack Confidential**. In 2005 it looks forward to the world premieres of **The Spirit of the Man** a commission from Stephen Lowe (about Brian Clough) and **Children of the Crown** by Nick Wood. And in 2005 it co-produces with Ipswich New Wolsey, Birmingham Repertory Theatre, Northern Stage ensemble and the Octagon Theatre, Bolton. Nottingham Playhouse is delighted to be co-producing the premiere of Amanda Whittington's **Satin 'n' Steel**, in association with Theatre Writing Partnership.

For more information on our work see **www.nottinghamplayhouse.co.uk.**

Chief Executive
Stephanie Sirr

Artistic Director
Giles Croft

Production Manager
D Sawyerr

Head of Finance & Administration
Rachael Thomas

Head of Marketing & Development
Sally Anne Tye

Director of Roundabout & Education
Andrew Breakwell

Photo courtesy of Martine Hamilton Knight

Nottingham Playhouse's work is made possible with the help and support of:

Nottinghamshire County Council

GEDLING
BOROUGH COUNCIL

Rushcliffe

Education Department
A♦B
Arts & Business

Nottingham Playhouse is the only UK member of the European Theatre Convention

Nottingham Playhouse

Wellington Circus
Nottingham
NG1 5AL

Box Office   0115 941 9419
Minicom   0115 947 6100
Fax   0115 924 1484

www.nottinghamplayhouse.co.uk

enquiry@nottinghamplayhouse.co.uk

Photo: Robert Day

The following companies support the work of Nottingham Playhouse through sponsorship of major projects, individual productions and support in kind, or through our corporate membership scheme, *in*BUSINESS.

Thanks to our business partners:

Sponsors
The Ark Day Nursery
Bentley Jennison
Childs Play Nursery
Derbyshire Building Society
De Facto
Experian
Hello Telecom
Hoofers Gym Dance & Fitness
Midland Mainline
Pennine Telecom
Presence - The Internet Specialists
Russell Scanlan Insurance
The University of Nottingham

***in*BUSINESS members**
Barclays Bank Plc
Browne Jacobson
Edwards Geldard Solicitors
IBM (UK) Ltd
Orchid (UK) Ltd

***in*HOUSE Business**
The Bookcase
Regent Street Dental Practice
Goodman East Midlands
Financial Services
Tomkins Florists

Lifestyle
Premier Travel Inn

octagon
Bolton

Co-Producer, Satin 'n' Steel

The Octagon Theatre, Bolton is widely regarded as one of the finest regional theatres in the UK.

"The increasingly confident Octagon...offers a programme of considerable breadth and depth"
The Guardian

Over 120,000 people visit the Octagon each year and make use of its facilities. The theatre produces eight to nine main stage productions per year and welcomes a variety of UK touring theatre companies including the National Theatre, John Godber's Hull Truck Theatre Company, Sir Alan Ayckbourn's Stephen Joseph Theatre and Out of Joint amongst others.

When the Octagon opened in 1967, it featured a ground-breaking design; the flexible auditorium offers a unique combination of spaces - end on, in-the-round, thrust and others. The Octagon's producing programme includes a vibrant range of contemporary, classic and new plays; World Premieres at the Octagon have included **Two** and **Bed** by Jim Cartwright, **Martha, Josie And The Chinese Elvis** by Charlotte Jones, **Pat And Margaret** by Victoria Wood, and, in 2001, the award-winning **Rat Pack Confidential** by Shawn Levy, another Octagon Theatre / Nottingham Playhouse co-production; also a national tour of **The Glee Club** (a co-production with the Bush Theatre). The Octagon's Studio Theatre is used to present a varied programme of new work, culturally diverse work, and events for and by young people, including performances by the Octagon's Youth Theatre.

activ8, the participation wing of the Octagon, has pioneered community, outreach and education programmes for a range of communities in the local area, especially those that are disadvantaged. Their work has become a benchmark for quality and success in the region.

The Octagon has been one of the most garlanded theatres at the Manchester Evening News Theatre Awards over the last four years, being nominated 45 times and winning nine major awards. The theatre has developed successful co-productions with partners including: Out Of Joint, York Theatre Royal, the Bush Theatre, Pilot Theatre, and of course two with Nottingham Playhouse. Audiences have increased by 20% over the last three years and the profile of the Octagon is rising, both regionally and nationally. The theatre strives to fulfil its mission, which is:
"to use our unique resources to make unforgettable theatre experiences that give pleasure, stimulate, challenge and enrich the lives of our communities and help release their creative potential".

For further information visit
www.octagonbolton.co.uk.

Executive Director: John Blackmore
Artistic Director: Mark Babych
Head of Production: Ben Monks
Head of Marketing: Lesa Dryburgh

The Octagon Theatre
Howell Croft South
Bolton
BL1 1SB

Ticket Office   01204 520661
General Enquiries   01204 529407

Registered Charity Number 248833

Theatre Writing Partnership (TWP) is a pioneering new writing organisation that started its life in February 2001.

Unique to the East Midlands region, it was set up to enable a greater creative collaboration on the development of new theatre writing across the producing theatres (Derby Playhouse, Leicester Haymarket, New Perspectives, Northampton's Royal and Derngate Theatres, and Nottingham Playhouse). The effect of this shared approach has been to enable the companies to develop pieces of work and relationships with artists in completely new ways. The production of **Satin 'n' Steel** at Nottingham Playhouse is a very good example of how this has worked successfully in reality.

Staged originally as part of **Get Shortie** (a season of short plays that were produced as curtain-raisers at the theatres in 2002) **Satin 'n' Steel** was part of the very first project that TWP pursued as an independent producer. **Get Shortie** enabled TWP, the participating theatres and writers to test out a completely new way of working and to introduce a range of voices to a diverse regional audience. Although all the plays in the season were well received, **Satin 'n' Steel** made a special impact. Amanda, Esther and the actors were keen to develop the play without the pressure to produce it at a particular time or in a particular context. Thanks to the Arts Council, our consortium of theatres and Nottingham Playhouse in particular, we have been able to pursue a unique developmental process. We have also been fortunate to sustain the involvement of almost all of the artists who contributed to the original production.

All TWP's independent initiatives are invariably events and projects that the theatres would be unlikely to pursue themselves as part of their regular turnover of productions. Our work therefore includes small-scale events and productions, writers' laboratories and workshops as well as the ongoing script-reading service and dramaturgical support that we provide to the theatres. Our credits include: **Momentum**, our young writers' project and festival which won this year's Peggy Ramsey Award; **Season of Courage**, which enabled six writers to create and present a 'statement of courage' to the audience before performances of **Mother Courage and Her Children**; the nationally acclaimed **Eclipse Writers' Lab**; and the studio-scale tour of **Riding the Rollercoaster**. We have also provided dramaturgical support on numerous productions across the region including: **Bollywood Jane** (Amanda Whittington), **The Palace of Fear** (Philip Osment), **The Illustrious Corpse** (Tariq Ali), **Mother Courage and Her Children** (Oladipo Agboluaje) and the forthcoming production of **Fortune Club** (Dolly Dhingra).

For further information, please contact Esther Richardson or Sarah Françoise on 0115 947 4361 or email esther@theatrewritingpartnership.com

SATIN 'N' STEEL

Amanda Whittington

Acknowledgements

Thank you to all those involved in the creative development of *Satin 'n' Steel*: Esther Richardson, Sara Poyzer, Norman Pace, Helen Davies, Stuart Briner, Giles Croft, Stephanie Sirr, David Walker, Mark Whiteley, Meg Davis, Nick Hern, Adam Wilde, Gina Reeves, Warren Tate and Arts Council East Midlands.

4

Characters

VINCE STEEl, *a club singer*

TEENA SATIN, *his protégée*

The play begins in present-day north Nottinghamshire.

This text went to press before the opening night and may differ slightly from the version as performed.

Note on Music

The script suggests a number of songs featured in Satin 'n' Steel's act. They could be changed if the rights to certain songs are unavailable, and the montage in Act One Scene Four could be replaced by a single song.

ACT ONE

Scene One

Miners' Welfare Club. November 2004. 5pm. VINCE STEEL
*(45) is a club singer who wears the dream of fame and fortune
like a cheap suit. He is setting up two microphones on stage.
When testing one, his voice echoes around the empty hall.*

VINCE. One-two-one-two-one-two. Good evening, Ren'oth,
how y' doing?

The microphone falters. VINCE *shakes it, slaps it and tries
again.*

He doesn't realise TEENA SATIN *(34) is watching from the
back of the hall. She wears a fur coat and an air of gritty
glamour.* VINCE *tries the microphone again.*

You know, a long time ago, when I was just a little-bitty
boy on Mama's knee, I said, 'Mama, I wanna be a big man.
I wanna have a big house and a big car and a big ol' pile of
money in the bank.' And you know what my mama said to
me? Well, this is what she said.

Than'youverymuch.

TEENA. Vince.

Beat.

VINCE. Teena.

I were just . . .

TEENA. S'all right. Sound-check.

Beat.

VINCE. You got the message then?

TEENA. Yeh.

VINCE. 'Cos I weren't sure, you know?

TEENA. I got it.

Beat.

VINCE. You look fantastic.

TEENA. Ta.

VINCE. When d'you do that, then? Your hair?

TEENA. Can't remember.

VINCE. Looks fantastic.

TEENA. Ta.

VINCE. Well, come on then, come up.

TEENA *comes onto the stage, somewhat reluctantly.* VINCE *speaks through the microphone.*

Ladies and gentle –

The microphone falters.

TEENA. New gear, you said.

VINCE. It's on order.

TEENA. Still?

VINCE. So where've you been, then?

TEENA. Oh, you know . . . around.

VINCE. Today, I mean. I said to get here by four.

TEENA. A lorry shed its load at Shirebrook.

VINCE. Shirebrook?

TEENA. Dog food.

VINCE. I said A60.

TEENA. Still in tins, like.

VINCE. In the message – A60, A617.

TEENA. My phone's playing up. Musta cut that bit off.

VINCE. And what if it had cut me off wholesale?

TEENA. It didn't.

VINCE. But what if it did? We could have lost a booking.

TEENA. But we didn't, did we?

VINCE. No. On this occasion, no.

TEENA. It cuts you off when you go on, that's all.

VINCE. I don't go on.

TEENA. I never said you did.

VINCE. I know, I know, I know. Point taken, subject closed.

TEENA. Good.

Beat.

VINCE. But I'd get yourself a new 'un all the same.

TEENA. Vince, I –

VINCE. Try her now.

TEENA *puts her car keys on the amp and takes the microphone.*

TEENA. It's the duff 'un, this.

VINCE. Let's have 'Wind Beneath Me Wings'.

TEENA. Where's the good 'un? I marked it with Gaffer.

VINCE. The showstopper, come on.

TEENA (*into the microphone*). Macaroni, macaroni.

VINCE. Give it some welly, Tee.

TEENA. Macaroni cheese.

VINCE. It just needs a bit of TLC, that's all.

VINCE *takes the microphone from her and gives it a slap.*

TEENA. So who dropped out then?

VINCE. You what, luv?

TEENA. Tonight. Someone must have dropped out.

VINCE. Nah, we've been booked in for weeks.

TEENA. So how come you didn't call me before?

VINCE. Oh aye, well, they might have mentioned someone.
Boy/girl duo. I think he called 'em Pazzazz.

TEENA. We saw them, Pazzazz.

VINCE. Did we?

TEENA. The lad's got a look of Robbie Williams.

VINCE. Oh?

TEENA. He had summat, that lad.

VINCE. Aye, a big head and a lot to learn. He called the old
boy here this morning, right? Announces he's got double
money up in Rochdale.

TEENA. He's got to earn a crust.

VINCE. There's more to life than money, Tee.

TEENA. Not when you've got none.

VINCE. In this game your word is your bond. There'll be no
more Pazzazz in these parts, I can tell you.

TEENA (*looking around*). Dead right.

VINCE (*into the microphone*). Ladies and gentlemen . . . Satin
'n' Stee –

It cuts out yet again.

TEENA. I told you it's the duff 'un.

VINCE. So where's the good 'un?

TEENA. Don't look at me; that's your department.

VINCE. It's just a loose connection. Hey now, there's a name
to conjure with: Loose Connection!

TEENA. Vince –

VINCE. We'll get renamed, remixed and repackaged. New
outfits, new photos now you've done your hair –

TEENA. So where is he, then? The boy wonder.

VINCE. We'll have an all-new top-class show.

TEENA. With top money and a top ten hit? Yeh, we're in the fast lane, us.

Beat.

VINCE. I had hoped we could be professional about all this.

TEENA. And just forget the fact you left me for –

VINCE. Just leave it, all right? We're here to do a show. A very important show as it happens.

Beat.

And you left me as I recall.

TEENA. Oh, I did, did I –

VINCE. Not tonight, Tee.

TEENA. And what's special about tonight, ey?

VINCE. Earth to Teena? It's our comeback show.

TEENA. Comeback? They rang you this morning.

VINCE hands her a scrap of paper.

VINCE. Set list.

TEENA. We don't open with 'Imagine'.

VINCE. It's me topical twist.

TEENA. Listen, Vince –

VINCE. No, you listen. I've given it a beat.

VINCE puts on a backing track of 'Imagine' by John Lennon. It is a ludicrously upbeat arrangement of the song.

TEENA. Christ . . .

VINCE. Come on, give it a go.

TEENA. It's a ballad.

VINCE. Not in our hands. Take it away.

VINCE *sings with total conviction. After a few bars,*
TEENA *joins in. She automatically falls into the harmonies*
and dance steps they perfected years before. Then she
comes to her senses and switches it off.

TEENA. Vince, it's ridiculous.

VINCE. We'll work on it. We'll go daring and adventurous.

TEENA. You're good at that.

VINCE. It'll be just like the old days. You and me together, we
were dynamite –

TEENA. We were Lipgloss.

VINCE. I'm not talking names. I'm talking ideas, energy,
passion.

TEENA. Well, you can pack that in 'cos I'm spoken for.

VINCE. Oh?

TEENA. Yeh. *(Beat.)* I've met a very nice man called Clive.

VINCE. What's his stage name?

TEENA. He's a plumber, Vince. He's not in the business.

VINCE. Oh. Sorry.

TEENA. Don't be. We're blissfully happy, thank you very
much.

VINCE. I mean I'm sorry for . . . It's just being up here with
you. I feel like a young man again.

TEENA. I wouldn't say that if you want to keep working.

Beat.

VINCE. Go on, get your slap on. We'll be on in a bit.

TEENA. I'm not going on.

VINCE. Come on, look lively. You can't stop the music –

TEENA. Vince! I've come here to tell you I'm not going on.

VINCE. Look, I didn't mean to . . . Well, we're both keyed up,
aren't we? Comeback show an' all that?

TEENA. I'm not coming back. Not after . . . Not this time.

Beat.

VINCE. Are you winding me up?

TEENA. I've got a job in a nursing home. Springfields, you know, on the ring road? I'm Senior Care Assistant.

VINCE. You're winding me up.

TEENA. I like it. I like the people. I start my shift in half an hour.

VINCE. You've turned up here to tell me that?

TEENA. Yeh.

VINCE *hands her his mobile phone.*

VINCE. Ring 'em. Tell 'em you've got one of your heads.

TEENA. I don't get heads.

VINCE. They don't know that. Ring 'em.

TEENA. I can't. We're short-staffed.

VINCE. They can do without you for a night.

TEENA. But I can't do without the money. It's regular, Vince. It's summat to rely on.

VINCE. You can rely on me.

TEENA *turns to go.*

TEENA. I'm sorry.

VINCE. Teena?

TEENA. I've got to go to work.

VINCE. But don't they know who you are?

TEENA. Yeh: I'm Tina White and I'm late.

VINCE. You're Teena Satin –

TEENA. Don't phone me any more.

VINCE. You're Teena Satin!

TEENA. *Was* Teena Satin.

VINCE. Oh, I get it. I see. You're too good for us now?

TEENA. You're right. Christ, is that the time? I'm on at Earls
Court at nine.

VINCE. So what did they learn you in London, then? Stage
fright.

TEENA. You've got no idea what frightens me. You never had.

Beat.

VINCE. So that's it? You're just giving up?

TEENA. I can't live on hope, Vince.

VINCE. I bet Jane McDonald never said that.

TEENA. It's over. We're over.

VINCE. Up and down the A1 in that old tranny van? Do them
years of sacrifice mean nothing?

TEENA. Don't you dare talk to me about sacrifice! Just don't.

VINCE. So what happened to the girl with the dream?

TEENA. She woke up and found you with the boy next door.

TEENA *walks out.*

VINCE. Teena? Teena, get back here now. Teena!

Beat.

Go on, then, go. I'll do it on my own. It's how you take
the knocks, that's what makes you a star. I don't need you,
I don't need no one. I can do it on my own. I've done it
before and I was all right. I was good. I was the Vince Steel
Experience. I was rock 'n' roll!

Scene Two

Miners' Welfare Club. April 1997. Midnight. VINCE (now 38) performs 'Johnny B Goode' by Chuck Berry. He has presence and charisma, and works the audience like a pro. He brings the song to a dynamic climax.

VINCE. Thank you! Than'youverymuch! I'm the Vince Steel Experience and you've been a fantastic audience. Safe journey, folks. Take care now and please, don't drink and drive. Thank you!

As VINCE *packs up his PA,* TEENA *(now 27) comes in from the main entrance. She is dressed for a big night out. She hurries in, finds her jacket and glances at* VINCE *on her way out.*

TEENA. I'll lose my bloody head next.

VINCE *watches her and waits until she's almost gone.*

VINCE. The glamour of showbiz.

TEENA. Ey?

VINCE. You won't get Robbie doing this.

TEENA. No.

VINCE. It's the side you don't see, in't it?

TEENA. Yeh.

VINCE. But I love it, me. This is what it's all about.

Beat.

TEENA. See you, then.

VINCE. Where are you off to?

TEENA. Home.

VINCE. You're not off celebrating?

TEENA. No.

VINCE. Not clubbin' it?

Beat.

TEENA. My boyfriend . . . He's waiting in the car.

VINCE. So what did he think?

TEENA. Of what?

VINCE. Tonight. What did he think of you?

TEENA. Oh . . . He's just picking us up.

VINCE. He weren't in?

TEENA. Nah.

VINCE. He didn't see you?

TEENA. No, I just came down with my mum.

VINCE. I bet she's proud of you, ey?

TEENA. Dunno.

VINCE. Come on, you did all right.

TEENA. Didn't win though, did I?

VINCE. Only 'cos that lad had all his mates in.

TEENA. I know. I've seen him before; he sings all over.

VINCE. Karaoke?

TEENA. Yeh.

VINCE. He sounds like a karaoke singer.

Beat.

Vince Steel.

TEENA. Yeh, I know.

TEENA *shakes his hand.*

VINCE. What's your name again?

TEENA. Tina.

VINCE. Tina what?

TEENA. Tina White.

VINCE. So where do you sing, Tina White?

TEENA. Oh, y' know . . . In the bath.

VINCE. What? You've not got a spot or summat?

TEENA. As if . . . No . . . I'm an overlocker, me. At Meritina.

VINCE. An overlocker?

TEENA. Yeh.

VINCE. So what do you overlock?

TEENA. Lingerie. All sorts.

VINCE. Lingerie?

TEENA. And other stuff. Skirts and tops an' that.

VINCE. And d'you like it?

TEENA. It's all right. It's a job. We have a laugh.

VINCE. I heard they're laying off, Meritina?

TEENA. They are, but I'm all right . . . for now . . . I think.

Beat.

Anyway . . .

VINCE. Can I ask you a question, Tina?

TEENA. If you want. If you're quick.

VINCE. You've got a fella, a job; you seem happy with your lot.

TEENA. I am.

VINCE. So how come you went up for the contest?

TEENA. I didn't. I could have killed me mum when you called out my name.

VINCE. So why d'you go through with it?

TEENA. Er . . . The fifty-quid prize.

VINCE. You did well, you know.

TEENA. I were pissed.

VINCE. No. You were good.

They hear a car horn.

TEENA. That's Trevor.

VINCE. Boy racer, is he?

TEENA. No, he's just . . . He's got my mum in the car, I'd better . . .

VINCE. Tell you what? I'll run you home.

TEENA. You're all right –

VINCE *gives* TEENA *a ten-pound note.*

VINCE. Get yourself a drink while you're waiting.

TEENA. No, ta.

VINCE. Go on, have what you want, I won't be long.

TEENA. I said no.

Beat.

VINCE. I don't want to shag you, luv.

TEENA. Er, likewise.

VINCE. I just want a little word.

TEENA. Well, here's one for you: bye.

TEENA *turns to go.*

VINCE. How come you knew the song?

TEENA. What song?

VINCE. The one you sang tonight, 'Wind Beneath My Wings'. If your mum sprung the contest on you, how come you knew it?

TEENA. Everyone knows it.

VINCE. Not like that.

Beat.

TEENA. Well, like I said, I sing in the bath.

VINCE. I'd like to hear it again.

TEENA. I bet you would.

VINCE. And in the right key this time.

TEENA. What do you mean, 'key'?

VINCE. I'd like to hear you sing it proper, with proper back-up. With someone who knows what they're doing.

TEENA. Like who?

VINCE. Like the region's top personality vocalist.

TEENA. You?

VINCE. What's funny?

TEENA. Me sing with you? Yeh, right . . .

VINCE. Why not? I've got a top-shelf set-up.

TEENA. A what?

VINCE. Do you wanna sing with me, Tina? Yes or no.

Beat.

TEENA. No.

VINCE. Why not?

TEENA. 'Cos you're professional and I'm crap.

VINCE. You're right. I am professional –

TEENA. Yeh –

VINCE. And you're not –

TEENA. Exactly –

VINCE. Crap.

TEENA. Oh.

VINCE. You've got summat, you have.

TEENA. Yeh, an 'eadache and a pissed-off boyfriend in the car.

VINCE. And has he never told you? Has no one ever said?

TEENA. No. Well, just my mum, but you know, that's just my mum.

VINCE. Well, I'm telling you, Tina. You've got it. You're a natural.

Beat.

What?

TEENA. This is Ren'orth. Night, Vince.

TEENA *turns to go.*

VINCE. So what do you earn at Meritina?

TEENA. That's my business.

VINCE. What do you think I got tonight?

TEENA. That's yours.

VINCE. Come on, have a guess before you go.

TEENA. How do I know?

VINCE. Guess.

TEENA. I dunno . . . fifty quid.

VINCE. I sang a few songs. Told a few jokes. Introduced the talent. (*Beat.*) Two hundred quid; and I'm gigging all over. Kirkby, Leabrooks, Clowne. As far as Burnley, Scarborough, Hull. A month today, I do the golf club up the road. Do you know it?

TEENA. I've passed it on the bus.

VINCE. Ninety minutes. Four hundred and fifty.

TEENA. Pounds?

VINCE. Now, Tina. Here's my proposition –

TEENA. You're not asking me to sing at the golf club? No. No way. No, no, no, no, no.

VINCE. No.

TEENA. Oh.

VINCE. I'm not asking you to sing at the golf club. But I am inviting you to join the Vince Steel Experience at The Saracen's Head on Tuesday week.

TEENA. Now hang on –

VINCE. Special guest spot. Three songs.

TEENA. I don't know three songs.

VINCE. You know 'Wind Beneath My Wings'.

TEENA. Yeh, I know the words but I don't 'four-hundred-quid' know it.

VINCE. All right, what do you think you're worth? How much?

Fifty quid a song?

TEENA. No.

VINCE. Twenty?

TEENA. No.

VINCE. Ten? Are you worth ten quid a song?

TEENA. Perhaps if I practised loads but –

VINCE. I'll give you thirty.

TEENA. A song?

VINCE. Yeh, thirty for the night. Cash-in-hand. I'll pick you up, drop you off. I'll take care of everything.

TEENA. Look, it's dead nice of you, but –

VINCE. We'll do Kiki Dee and Elton – 'Don't Go Breaking My Heart' – and 'I Got You Babe', I bet you know that one. We'll rehearse 'em next week.

TEENA. I can't next week.

VINCE. Monday night. Eight o'clock.

TEENA. Vince? I can't.

Beat.

VINCE. Fine . . . No problem . . . I'm not gonna push it . . . If you don't want to do it . . .

VINCE returns to his packing-up.

TEENA. Why don't you ask that lad? Vince? I know where you can find him.

VINCE. No.

TEENA. But he was the winner.

VINCE. I know he was. But I want you.

TEENA. You're taking the piss.

VINCE. You are. Bloody overlocking all your life.

TEENA. Oh, and who are you to tell me how to live?

VINCE. I'm Vince Steel, and I know a voice when I hear one.

The car horn sounds again, loud and angry. VINCE *looks at* TEENA, *waiting for an answer.* TEENA *hesitates.*

TEENA. No.

TEENA leaves the club. VINCE *returns to packing his gear. He winds the leads up quickly and throws them into the box when* TEENA *comes back in.*

Thirty quid?

VINCE. That's what I said.

Beat.

TEENA. Thirty quid a song.

VINCE. Has your fella put you up to this?

TEENA. He's buggered off, an't he, thanks to you. (*Beat.*) Three songs. Ninety quid.

VINCE. Fifty quid.

TEENA. I want to take my mum to Ingoldmells. Eighty.

VINCE. Fifty pound for an hour's work. Do you get that at Meritina?

Beat.

TEENA. S'all right, I've changed my mind.

VINCE. Why?

TEENA. 'Cos my boyfriend won't like it.

VINCE. Nor will mine, but this is business.

Beat.

TEENA. I'd never have known.

VINCE. So have we got a deal or what?

TEENA *puts out her hand.*

TEENA. Three songs. Sixty quid.

VINCE *takes it.*

VINCE. Done.

Scene Three

Golf Club. Backstage. May 1997. 9pm. VINCE wears a shirt and boxer shorts, and is warming up his voice.

VINCE. Me-me-me-me-me-me-me-me-me.

TEENA *comes into the dressing room in a cocktail dress. Seeing him half-dressed, she turns back to leave the room.*

TINA. Sorry.

VINCE. Ha-ha-ha-ha-ha-ha-ha.

TEENA. What?

VINCE. Nowt, I'm warming up.

TEENA. Do I have to warm up?

VINCE. You're red hot already.

TEENA. Is my dress all right?

VINCE. Ah-aaah-aahhhh!

TEENA. I ran it up at work. It's what you wanted? Vince?

VINCE. Tina White. Dressed to kill, licensed to thrill.

TEENA. You won't say that when I come on?

VINCE. Waaaahhh!

TEENA. You'll tell 'em it's my first time?

VINCE. So what do you call The Saracen's Head?

TEENA. A shithole.

VINCE. And the Labour Club, and the Legion?

TEENA. But it's my first time proper. Vince, I think you should warn 'em.

VINCE. Do you want 'L' plates an' all?

Beat.

TEENA. Just don't do one of your big build-ups.

VINCE. I won't.

TEENA. Promise?

VINCE. Cross my heart and hope to die. I'll just say summat like, 'Ladies and gentlemen, I've got a fantastic guest singer. She's just come back from a six-month cruise, she's entertained around the world, she's sung for Danish royalty – '

TEENA. No!

VINCE. You're not nervous, are you?

TEENA. No, Vince, I'm not nervous, I'm shitting it.

VINCE. Breathe and smile, that's all you've got to do. Breathe and smile like I showed you. Go on.

TEENA. Breathe and smile.

VINCE. Give a big wave to your mum sat at the back.

TEENA. She's at bingo.

VINCE. I know: it's visualation. Breathe and smile.

TEENA. Breathe and smile.

VINCE. Breathe and smile.

TEENA. My lips are sticking to my teeth.

VINCE. Don't forget what I said about the mike. Hold it firm but not in front of your face.

TEENA. Firm.

VINCE. Shoulders down, chin up and go where the music takes you, right?

TEENA. Right.

VINCE. That's my girl. *(Beat.)* And watch your step when you come out. They've left the darts platform up.

TEENA. The what?

TEENA *goes to look through the curtain.*

VINCE. Not in your costume! Bloody hell.

TEENA. I'm only looking.

VINCE. Well, don't. It's not professional.

TEENA. It's not professional to go arse over tit when you come on.

VINCE. Does my hair look all right?

TEENA. Yeh.

VINCE. Does it?

TEENA. Does mine?

VINCE. Spray it again; you'll be surprised how you sweat.

TEENA *sprays her hair.*

TEENA. Vince?

VINCE. Mmmmmmmmm.

TEENA. You won't say that Danish royalty thing, will you?

VINCE. Rarararararararararara.

TEENA. 'Cos I don't care what you say – I'm not a professional.

VINCE. Who's been rehearsing every night this week?

TEENA. Me.

VINCE. Who sung perfect at the sound-check?

TEENA. You.

VINCE. And who'll pocket four hundred smackers for tonight?

TEENA. Me and you.

VINCE. See? You're a pro.

VINCE *stands on a chair to put on his trousers.*

TEENA. What are you doing?

VINCE. Little tip I got off Frank.

TEENA. Sinatra?

VINCE. Carson. Keeps the crap off the floor off your trousers.

TEENA. Vince –

VINCE (*as Frank Carson*). It's the way I tell 'em.

TEENA. Can I just have a quick look for the dart thing?

VINCE. I worked with him, you know? Frank Carson. I gave him that catchphrase.

TEENA. Can I?

Beat.

VINCE. All right, all right. I'll show yer how it's done.

TEENA. Ta.

VINCE. Pull the curtain back like so.

VINCE *discreetly pulls back the curtain.*

See? It's just a little slope, look. Once you've set it in your head, you'll be . . .

TEENA. What?

VINCE. Bloody hell.

TEENA. What?

VINCE. Bloody hellfire . . .

TEENA. Have they raised it up or summat? Vince, what is it?

VINCE *closes the curtain.*

VINCE. Bernard Matthews.

TEENA. Who?

VINCE. Bernard Matthews.

TEENA. The turkey bloke?

VINCE. No, Tina. *The* Bernard Matthews. The biggest variety agent in the Midlands.

TEENA *(laughs)*. Bernard Matthews, is that really his name?

VINCE. It's not funny. We're talking Mr Entertainment. He's corporates and cruises and not just them crap 'uns on the North Sea neither.

TEENA. What? Like in Barbados?

VINCE. All over.

TEENA. He gets singers on cruise ships?

VINCE. That's what I said.

TEENA. And he's come here tonight to see us?

VINCE. Either that or he's a golfer.

TEENA. Oh my God, that's fantastic. That's brilliant!

VINCE. In't it.

TEENA. In't it?

Beat.

VINCE. Yeh.

TEENA. So what's up?

VINCE. Nowt.

TEENA. What's wrong, d'you get seasick or summat?

VINCE. No.

TEENA. So what's the matter?

VINCE. Bloody Bernard Matthews, that's what. He's six months too soon.

TEENA. What do you mean?

VINCE. What do you think? We're not ready.

Beat.

TEENA. You mean I'm not ready?

VINCE. I never said that.

TEENA. It's all right. You don't have to.

TEENA *starts packing up her stuff.*

VINCE. Where d'you think you're going?

TEENA. To meet me mam –

VINCE. Tina –

TEENA. Her leg's playing up. I'll walk her home –

VINCE. Come on, don't take the 'ump.

TEENA. I'm not.

VINCE. All I meant was it's our first proper gig. Even Dolly and Kenny woulda warmed up.

TEENA. Well, I'm not Dolly Parton. You've made that obvious.

VINCE. Oh, I see? I get it. You've bottled it.

TEENA. Get lost.

VINCE. You've made a few quid, you've had a laugh but when the going gets tough –

TEENA. Don't talk to me about tough –

VINCE. When the going gets tough, the tough go to bingo.

TEENA. Piss off, Vince.

VINCE. I thought you had backbone, you. I thought you had guts.

TEENA. Well, you thought wrong. Barbados? I'm Tina White from Ren'orth and I should have known better.

VINCE. What's white in French?

TEENA. You what?

VINCE. Vin rouge and vin . . .

TEENA. Blanc.

VINCE. Right. You're Tina Vin Blanc. If Tina White can't do it, she can.

TEENA. I'm not changing me name.

VINCE. You're not leaving this dressing room neither.

TEENA. Dressing room? It's a corridor.

VINCE. Tina Snow.

TEENA. Shift.

VINCE. Tina Sunshine?

TEENA. Tina the Cleaner. I could go on with a mop.

VINCE. Spell Tina with a double 'e' – that goes good with Steel.

TEENA. No ta, they'll think we're married.

VINCE. Steel Diamond?

TEENA. Stainless Steel.

VINCE. Steely Thunders, how about that?

TEENA. It sounds like a fart.

VINCE. Got you smiling though, didn't it?

TEENA. No.

VINCE. That's all you've got to do, luv. Breathe and smile; breathe and smile; breathe and smile and sing your heart out for Vince. Please?

Beat.

TEENA. Tina White. 'Tis a crap name.

VINCE. So what's a good 'un? What's the opposite of steel? Come on, think. Steel and . . .

TEENA. Sugar?

VINCE. No.

TEENA. Silk?

VINCE. No.

TEENA. Satin?

VINCE. Steel and Satin . . .

TEENA. Satin and Steel?

VINCE. Satin and Steel . . . Sounds like Sapphire and Steel, but that's good, that's the hook.

TEENA. Sounds stupid to me.

VINCE. Well, have you got owt better?

TEENA. I always thought Lipgloss was a good name for a group.

VINCE. Lipgloss?

TEENA. It sounds sorta glamorous. I like it.

VINCE. Bernard Matthews – meet Lipgloss.

TEENA. Is that his real name?

VINCE. Well, you wouldn't pick it, would yer?

TEENA. Or pluck it.

VINCE. No turkey jokes, Teena with a double 'e'.

TEENA. I'll make 'em if I want to, Vince with a 'V'.

TEENA *gives* VINCE *a V-sign.*

VINCE. Bootiful. You are, you know?

TEENA. Oh, shut up and show us where he's sat.

VINCE. See the fat bloke in the Pringle top?

VINCE *pulls back the curtain.*

TEENA. Which one?

VINCE. With the chunky gold chain.

TEENA. Shit.

VINCE. I know, I bet it's worth a packet.

TEENA. Shit!

VINCE. What?

TEENA. Trevor's out there.

VINCE. Trevor who?

TEENA. Trevor my boyfriend wi' a big gang of mates.

VINCE. You never said he was coming.

TEENA. He weren't. I told him not to. I knew he'd do this,
I knew it!

Beat.

VINCE. Teena?

TEENA. What?

VINCE. You've not made out that me and you are –

TEENA. 'Course not. Bloody hell, as if.

VINCE. He's not after me, then?

TEENA. No.

VINCE. Are you sure about that?

TEENA. I told him all about it – all about us. And he laughed.

VINCE. What do you mean, 'laughed'?

TEENA. Me singing in public. He thinks it's pathetic. He's
come to take the piss.

VINCE. Right . . . Good.

TEENA. Well, I'm glad you're happy.

VINCE. He'll not do owt. He'll be knocked out when he sees
yer.

TEENA. He won't. He's . . . He's a twat.

VINCE. So what are you doing with him?

TEENA. Don't ask.

VINCE. Well, I am. Come on? What's a girl like you doing
with him? You're good-looking, hard-working, you're
funny –

TEENA. I must be.

VINCE. You've got everything going for you, Tee. Everything.
You've got the voice, the brains, the beauty, the wotsit . . .
The *parlez-vous-française* . . .

TEENA. *Je ne sais quoi.*

VINCE. See? You've got it. You've got it to burn. And I want
you to go out there tonight and set 'em on fire.

TEENA. I can't.

VINCE. Yes, you can, Teena.

TEENA. I can't. (*Beat.*) You don't know what he's like. He'll
start heckling and shouting and he'll make it all . . . He'll
spoil it.

VINCE. You think so?

TEENA. I know so. He's been all day in the pub –

VINCE. And who's been eighteen years in the business?
Who's played for squaddies out in Cyprus?

TEENA. Jesus Christ.

VINCE. No, Vince Steel. And if he starts on you, I'll have him.

TEENA. What do you mean?

VINCE. Let's just say, I've got the mike.

TEENA. You'll not hit him with it?

VINCE. No.

TEENA. You won't, will yer?

VINCE. Swear to Elvis. (*As Elvis.*) Uh-huh.

Beat.

TEENA. He's got a thing about me singing, Vince. He said that if I came here tonight then we're finished.

VINCE. And what did you say?

TEENA. I tried to tell him it were just a bit of fun.

VINCE. Is it?

TEENA. Well, not for you, I know that. *(Beat.)* So I think it's best if you do it without me.

VINCE. Teena . . .

TEENA. Please, Vince. You've got Bernard Matthews here and everything, and you've been great to me. Really, really great. And the last thing I wanna do is make you look a –

VINCE. You're the best thing that's happened to me in years. You know that, don't yer?

Beat.

TEENA. Get lost.

VINCE. We're going places, us. We're going all the way.

TEENA. Don't. Don't say things like that.

VINCE. Why not? You want it, don't yer?

Beat.

TEENA. You know I do.

Beat.

VINCE. Good. See you out there.

VINCE *leaves the dressing room.*

TEENA. Shit.

VINCE *(off)*. Ladies and gentlemen, I'd like to introduce a fantastic new singing sensation. They've just returned from a six-month cruise.

TEENA. Shit!

VINCE (*off*). They've entertained around the world, they've sung for Danish royalty and now they're here to sing for you tonight. So put your hands together please for Lipgloss!

Scene Four

Golf Club stage. VINCE *begins the show with an uptempo song, which soon segues into another. The medley moves through some of pop's most famous hooks and anthems.*

TEENA *joins in the medley. At first, she is nervous but led by* VINCE, *she grows in confidence. Their medley takes us through a jukebox of pop classics, from 'Crocodile Rock' to 'I Will Survive'.*

As the songs change, so do the venues, backdrops, seasons and costumes. We see the passage of time and the growth in their relationship. The songs are peppered with 'Good evening, Scunthorpe . . . Manton . . . Hull.'

VINCE. Ladies and gentlemen, I'm Vince Steel.

TEENA. And I'm Teena Satin.

VINCE. And together . . .

TEENA. We're Satin 'n' Steel!

As the medley builds, their song-and-dance routines become slicker until TEENA *begins to lead* VINCE.

A banner announces the appearance of Satin 'n' Steel as the headline act at Butlins. VINCE *and* TEENA *are at the top of their game. Their onstage chemistry is clear for all to see. They close the dynamic medley with a triumphant disco finish.*

TEENA. Thank you, Butlins – goodnight!

Scene Five

Butlins chalet. February 1998. 2am. VINCE *and* TEENA
crash into the chalet, in stage clothes. VINCE *has a bottle of
Asti Spumante and is wearing plastic 1970s star-shaped
glasses.*

TEENA. Oh Vince, oh Vince, oh Vince! How good was that?
Nine hundred people up and dancing.

VINCE. Teena, luv, you've sewn your last pair of pants.

VINCE *pops the cork as* TEENA *finds two teacups.*

TEENA. Oh God, it was brilliant! It was brilliant and fantastic
and amazing and –

VINCE. You were amazing.

TEENA. You were.

VINCE. You were amazinger.

TEENA. You were more amazinger.

VINCE. You even won the raffle.

TEENA. Everything we've worked on came right all at once.

VINCE. You're a top turn, Teena Satin.

TEENA. You're not so bad yourself, Vince Steel.

VINCE *pours the drinks.*

VINCE. To us.

VINCE / TEENA. Satin 'n' Steel!

TEENA. To free champagne.

VINCE. You've had more than three.

TEENA. To the future.

VINCE. To a thousand bloody quid!

TEENA. Less commission.

VINCE. To Bernie!

VINCE / TEENA. Bernard Matthews!

TEENA. To your glasses.

VINCE. Look good, don't they?

TEENA. They'd look better on me.

   TEENA *takes the glasses and puts them on.*

VINCE. I used to come to Butlins every summer as a kid. If they could see me now, ey? Back and topping the bill.

TEENA. In your VIP chalet.

VINCE. With champagne on tap.

TEENA. Tastes good in a teacup.

VINCE. It's better from the bottle.

   VINCE *drinks from the bottle.*

TEENA. Give it here.

   TEENA *drinks from the bottle.*

VINCE. Steady on.

TEENA. Oh, thank you, Vince. Thank you, thank you, thank you, thank you, thank you.

VINCE. Thank you, Teena Satin.

TEENA. What for?

VINCE. Oh, I'll tell you one day.

TEENA. Tell me now.

VINCE. No.

TEENA. Go on.

VINCE. I'm pissed.

TEENA. No, you're not. You're just a little drunk on our fantabulous success.

VINCE. Yeh, but don't get complacent. We've got to do it all again tomorrow.

TEENA. And the night after that and the night after that, for ever and ever and ever.

VINCE. You might even get it right by then.

TEENA. I never put a foot wrong, me.

VINCE. You missed the whole middle section out the rock-and-roll dance.

TEENA. You did.

VINCE. You did.

TEENA. I know that routine back to front.

VINCE. Well, you did it backwards tonight.

TEENA takes off the glasses.

TEENA. Did I? Did I really?

Beat.

VINCE. You were perfect.

TEENA. Oh Vince, it's been the best night of my life.

VINCE. Well, get used to it, Teena. There's plenty more to come.

TEENA. Let's go for a walk on the beach.

VINCE. It's slinging it down.

TEENA. So? Let's stay out all night and see the sun rise.

VINCE. We're in Skeg.

TEENA. We'll have candyfloss for breakfast.

VINCE. No!

TEENA. Come on, I want to see the sea.

VINCE. Darlin', you'll be cruising on it soon.

TEENA. No way!

VINCE. All Bernie's got to do is say the word. It's a life on the ocean wave for us, Tee.

TEENA. I can't believe it. I can't believe this is happening.

VINCE. Why? You've worked for it. You've earned it. You deserve it.

Beat.

TEENA. You know if we ever do do a cruise?

VINCE. You mean *when.*

TEENA. All right, *when* we do, can we take someone with us?

VINCE. Like who?

TEENA. I know it's not professional, but I'm thinking, my mum . . . She's never been abroad and she always said if she won the pools, that's what she'd do. She'd do a cruise.

VINCE. Can she play the bongos?

TEENA. No. I'd pay for her, though. I could afford it, too, the way things are going.

VINCE. Why d'you never bring her to the gigs?

TEENA. I will when I'm good enough. I want to make it special.

VINCE. She's special to you, in't she?

TEENA. 'Course she is; she's my mum.

VINCE. So what's she like?

TEENA. Ah, she's fantastic. She doesn't say much but she takes it all in. She might not look it, but she's strong, dead strong. She's had to be.

VINCE. How come?

TEENA. Oh, just stuff that went off . . . Do you want the sofa or the bed?

VINCE. What kind of stuff?

TEENA. Just with me dad. (*Beat.*) One bedroom. They must think we're having it away.

VINCE. Or we're an old married couple.

TEENA. Mr and Mrs Steel.

VINCE. Byczewski.

TEENA. Bless you.

VINCE. That's my name. My real name.

TEENA. What? Vince Bizooski?

VINCE. Victor.

TEENA. Vince Victor?

VINCE. Victor Byczewski. My dad's a Pole.

TEENA. My dad's a plank.

Beat.

VINCE. You don't have to tell us.

TEENA. No, you're all right. They all know up our way what
he was.

VINCE. He's not around, then?

TEENA. No, thank God, she kicked him out.

VINCE. Why's that?

TEENA. Oh 'cos he was drinking a litre of vodka a day and
hitting her and acting like a general wanker. Yeh . . . That's
partly why I'm still at home, I just want to be there for her,
you know. I couldn't do much about it, then . . . Well, I say
that, a couple of times I did swing for him myself but he's a
big bloke and he was pissed.

VINCE. You hit him?

TEENA. Yeh, one Christmas Eve. I was sixteen, I was sat
watching telly with my mum and he came in and he was
absolutely shit-faced. He started shouting and my mum was
shouting back, then he starts pushing her and she pushes
him back and then he grabbed her and I jumped on his
back. It was actually quite funny 'cos I was on his back and
my mum was at the front trying to push him off and it's like
'Merry Christmas', you know? He went to a clinic after that
and it was good, it was nice, I got my dad back for a while

and he's quite sweet when he's sober, he's an all-right kind of bloke. But then he started drinking again and finally, after eighteen years, my mum kicked him out. He could be dead for all I know, but anyway, my mum, you'll have to meet her. I've told her all about you.

VINCE. What have you said?

TEENA. Oh, just that you're a bit of an arse.

VINCE. Cheers.

TEENA. I didn't really.

Beat.

VINCE. So what did you say?

Beat.

TEENA. I talk too much, don't I?

VINCE. No.

TEENA. I do when I've had a few. You say summat.

VINCE. Like what?

TEENA. I dunno, anything.

VINCE. Ask us a question. Pretend you're Parkinson, come on.

Beat.

TEENA. What's your favourite colour?

VINCE. Red, Michael.

TEENA. What's your favourite thing to do?

VINCE. Sing.

TEENA. What's your favourite happy memory?

VINCE. Tonight on stage with you.

Beat.

TEENA. 'Tis a memory now, in't it?

VINCE. 'Til the next time, I'm telling you. It's just the beginning.

TEENA. I have got a question, Vince. Your fella . . . Neil . . . How come he never comes to the gigs?

VINCE. He just don't.

TEENA. Why?

VINCE. Well, he wouldn't take me to work, would he?

TEENA. What does he do?

VINCE. Does it matter?

TEENA. All right, I'm only asking.

Beat.

VINCE. He's not in the business.

TEENA. How long have you been with him, then?

VINCE. A while. A few years. I dunno.

TEENA. I think there's summat wrong with him. I think he's got an 'ump.

VINCE. You think too much.

TEENA. I want to see him, that's all. Is he lush?

VINCE. Lush?

TEENA. Has he seen me? Has he seen the ten-by-eights?

VINCE. Yeh.

TEENA. Did he say I looked tarty?

VINCE. No.

TEENA. He did, I can tell.

VINCE. Teena –

TEENA. Do you think I look tarty?

Beat.

VINCE. I think you look like Teena Satin.

TEENA. I felt like Teena Satin tonight.

VINCE. Well, don't get cocky. You messed up big-style or have you forgot?

TEENA. You messed up.

VINCE. You came in too early.

TEENA. You came in too late.

VINCE. It's this, in't it?

VINCE sings 'Don't Go Breaking My Heart' by Elton John and Kiki Dee. TEENA joins in but stops singing after a few lines.

VINCE. Go on.

TEENA. Are you ashamed of me, Vince? Do you think I'd show you up if I met him?

VINCE. 'Course not. Bloody hell, where's that come from?

TEENA. Are you ashamed of him, then? Is that why you never bring him?

VINCE. No.

TEENA. Are you ashamed of being gay?

VINCE. I'm not gay.

TEENA. Oh. Does your boyfriend know that?

VINCE. He's not my boyfriend as such. He doesn't live with me or owt, he's just . . . Well, I've had girlfriends, an't I? Loads of 'em. But now I've got him.

TEENA. And you don't have to hide it, not in this day and age. I mean, you know, there's Elton John. And Wayne, the lad from work, he's a right laugh.

VINCE. Teena, I'm an all-round entertainer.

TEENA. You can say that again.

VINCE. I'm Vince Steel, aren't I? And when Vince Steel's up there, he's Mr Showbiz. He's The Man. He's selling you a dream . . . And you can't sell 'em that dream. Not round here.

Boat.

TEENA. So is that why you've got me? To cover your tracks?
'Cos if it is, you can tell me. Tell me straight.

VINCE. So to speak.

TEENA. Is it?

VINCE. You know why I've got you. And I'm not letting go.

VINCE *puts his arms around* TEENA *and they cuddle up
together.*

TEENA. So what is your dream?

VINCE. What's yours?

TEENA. I'm asking you.

VINCE. I'm asking you.

TEENA. You're good at changing the subject, aren't you?

VINCE. Yeh. What's your dream?

Beat.

TEENA. Do you want a work dream or a me dream?

VINCE. A you dream.

TEENA. Apart from being a famous singer an' that . . . my
biggest dream's a house of my own. A two-bedroom terrace
down the road from my mum. You can pick 'em up for
twenty grand. I know it's rough but I'm not bothered. I'd do
it all up: red walls, wooden floors, a big zebra-print sofa.
I've seen one in town. Floaty curtains and white linen sheets
on a big iron bed, that's what I want.

VINCE. And a fella to go in it?

TEENA. Who needs a fella? I've got you.

VINCE. Have you now?

TEENA. And I can do this.

She hugs him.

And this.

She kisses him.

And I don't have to put up with your snoring.

VINCE. It's good to be loved.

TEENA. 'Tis good.

VINCE. Yeh . . .

TEENA. It's fantastic.

VINCE. I know.

TEENA. I've never met anyone like you, Vince.

VINCE. I know.

Beat.

TEENA. Don't look at me like that.

VINCE. Like what?

TEENA. Like you're Paul McKenna or summat.

VINCE. You – feel – sleepy.

TEENA. Go on . . . tell us your dream.

Beat.

VINCE. I'd get a motorbike. I'd get myself a great big *Easy Rider* Harley, put my foot down and go.

TEENA. Where?

VINCE. Dunno. Don't care. I'd find out when I get there.

TEENA. Right.

Beat.

VINCE. What?

TEENA. Nothing.

VINCE. No, come on, what's wrong with that?

TEENA. Nowt. I just thought you'd say making a record or some great big London show.

VINCE. That's not a dream. That's the future.

TEENA. Is it?

VINCE. Stick with me, kid; we're going all the way.

TEENA. I wish.

Beat.

VINCE. What are you thinking?

TEENA. You don't wanna know.

VINCE. Yes, I do. I want to know everything about you.

Beat.

TEENA. Your *Easy Rider* Harley. Is there room on the back?

Beat.

VINCE. Shall we stop talking now?

TEENA. You're right, yeh. It's late.

VINCE. Teena –

TEENA. No, come on, do you want the sofa or the bed?

VINCE. What do you want?

TEENA. Vince . . .

VINCE. It's all right. I know.

VINCE *goes to kiss* TEENA *but she stops him.*

TEENA. We can't.

VINCE. Yes, we can. You and me, we can do anything.

TEENA. No.

TEENA *goes into the bedroom.* VINCE *sits down then looks back, as if she might come in but she doesn't.* VINCE *finds a blanket and lies on the sofa to sleep.* TEENA *appears from the bedroom.*

TEENA. Vince? (*Beat.*) Sofa or bed?

VINCE *goes to her and they disappear into the bedroom.*

ACT TWO

Scene One

Stage. November 2002. 10pm. VINCE and TEENA perform 'Islands In The Stream' by Dolly Parton and Kenny Rogers. The act is now highly polished but TEENA appears to be going through the motions.

TEENA. Thanks.

   TEENA walks offstage.

VINCE. Thank you very much. Goodnight.

   VINCE follows TEENA.

Scene Two

Ferry deck. Minutes later. TEENA stands shivering in her stage clothes. She is holding something close to her, as if to keep her warm. VINCE comes onto the deck. TEENA ignores him.

VINCE. What are you doing?

   Silence.

You're not done yet, you know?

   Silence.

Come on, you've got the encore.

TEENA. What's happened, Vince?

VINCE. You walked offstage, that's what.

TEENA. I mean how did we end up here?

Beat.

VINCE. It's work, it's what we do.

TEENA. What? Play shit gigs to pissed people who sit looking up your skirt?

VINCE. I don't wear a skirt.

TEENA. Why can't I talk to Bernie? Why can't I get involved with the bookings? You never ask me what I want.

VINCE. I know what you want.

TEENA. You ring me up and say, 'Teena, pack your posh frocks, we're going on a cruise.'

VINCE. It is a cruise.

TEENA. I thought you meant like, you know, the QE2.

VINCE. You're on the water, aren't you?

TEENA. It's a North Sea ferry.

VINCE. All right, yeh, it's basic.

TEENA. There's sheep in the back.

VINCE. That's the engine, they all make that noise; and at least we're together.

TEENA. In bunk beds.

VINCE. Mine's comfy.

TEENA. Mine's crap.

Beat.

VINCE. It's one duff gig, that's all.

TEENA. What? Like Carlisle and Leatherhead and Filey and –

VINCE. We can't bring the house down every night.

TEENA. Vince, we're going nowhere. We're stuck on the circuit, we're going round in circles –

VINCE. Yeh, and we've got another song to do, come on.

TEENA. Oh, did I not say? I'm not singing no more.

VINCE. You're not what?

TEENA. You heard. I can't sing them songs like I mean 'em.

VINCE. Teena, this is showbiz, you don't have to mean 'em.

TEENA. I'm sorry, Vince, you'll have to do it on your own and
I tell you summat else: this time tomorrow, I won't be on
this boat.

VINCE. Ship.

TEENA. I'm packing me bags and getting off.

VINCE. How?

TEENA. I dunno, I'll get a lifeboat or summat.

VINCE. Oh, so you're gonna ask the Captain, are you?
'Excuse me, can you drop me off at bloody Croatia?'

TEENA. I want to go home. (*Beat.*) I've not left a light on. It's
rough up our end, if you don't leave a light on, they'll be in.

Beat.

VINCE. Teena luv –

TEENA. I said I'd take her on a cruise.

VINCE. I know you did.

TEENA. I promised. (*Beat.*) She'd never been no further than
Sutton-on-Sea. I raised her hopes.

Beat.

VINCE. See that star? That big bright one, just there? See it?
That's your mum that is, looking down –

TEENA. She's not up there. She's in here.

TEENA *gestures to the urn she's holding.*

VINCE. Shall we scatter 'em now then, ey? Get it over with?

Silence.

I mean, that's why you brought 'em.

Silence.

You can't hang on to 'em for ever, luv, come on.

VINCE *tries to take the urn but* TEENA *pushes him away.*

TEENA. Get off!

Beat.

VINCE. Teena, you can't go on like this. You've got to get a grip. I've bent over backwards but if you won't let me near you . . .

Silence.

I'm doing my best.

Silence.

I know what you need.

TEENA. What?

VINCE. A nice little holiday. We'll get some dates in Benidorm, I know a bloke –

TEENA. Send us a postcard.

VINCE. Teena . . .

TEENA. Adios, Vince.

Beat.

VINCE. I know what your mum'd say. 'The Show Must Go On.'

TEENA. The last thing she said to me was dump you.

VINCE. No, she never.

TEENA. She said, 'How would he feel if you were going home to Bob? If you were ironing his shirts and ringing him up: "Oh, I can't see you tonight, I'm staying in with Bob"?'

VINCE. Who's Bob?

TEENA. It doesn't matter who Bob is. What would you say if I was seeing someone else?

VINCE. You're not.

TEENA. Are you?

VINCE. I beg your pardon?

TEENA. Are you?

VINCE. No.

TEENA. So why won't you live with me?

VINCE. Not now, Teena.

TEENA. Why?

Beat.

VINCE. Look, if you want a Bob –

TEENA. I don't –

VINCE. If you want a normal bloke, who comes home every
    night –

TEENA. I don't want a normal bloke. I want you. I want to
    wake up with you; I want to bring you breakfast in bed; I
    want you there for birthdays and Christmas.

VINCE. You want to iron my shirts; and cook my tea; and fight
    about the bog seat and the bloody remote?

TEENA. Come home with me. Live with me. Be with me.

VINCE. I am with you.

TEENA. Not as Satin 'n' Steel: as Vince and Teena. As a proper
    full-on couple.

VINCE. And have you thought about the act? What'll happen
    to the act?

TEENA. Fuck the act! Fuck the act, and don't say I have, 'cos
    I'm sick of your stupid jokes and all.

VINCE. But we *are* the act. We're the spark, the chemistry, the
    magic.

TEENA. So is that why you're with me? Is that why we're
    together?

VINCE. No.

TEENA. You're lying.

VINCE. Am I?

TEENA. Where were you Monday?

VINCE. You what?

TEENA. You heard. Where were you Monday night?

VINCE. Monday . . .

TEENA. Have you met someone else?

VINCE. 'Course not.

TEENA. So who did you sneak off to phone this morning?

VINCE. Bernie.

TEENA. At seven o'clock?

VINCE. Our time, not his.

TEENA. You're shagging someone else.

VINCE. When have I got time for someone else? I'm with you
    every night.

TEENA. You weren't on Monday.

VINCE. I went for a drink.

TEENA. Who with?

VINCE. We're halfway through a show here.

TEENA. I phoned you. I phoned at three in the morning,
    where were you?

VINCE. In bed.

TEENA. Who with?

VINCE. For the last time, Teena, there's no other woman.

TEENA. Is there a man?

    Beat.

VINCE. No.

TEENA. Is it Neil?

VINCE. No.

TEENA. Are you back with him? Are you?

VINCE. No!

TEENA. You're never gonna love me. We're never gonna make it. This is all we are and all we're ever gonna be.

The tannoy calls for Satin 'n' Steel in Norwegian.

VINCE. I think that's us.

TEENA. A two-bit turn on a North Sea ferry.

VINCE. Not forever.

TEENA. Six years, you've been saying that.

VINCE. Six of the best, though. Well, they have been for me.

Beat.

TEENA. Monday night, I just sat there in the flat by the phone. No lights, no music, no nothing.

VINCE. Hey, you're Teena Satin. You're a star, a shining star.

TEENA. I don't feel shiny any more.

Beat.

VINCE. Come here.

TEENA. No.

VINCE. Come on . . .

VINCE puts his arms around her, knocking the urn.

TEENA. Careful.

VINCE. It's all right . . . it's all right . . . we're nearly done . . . I'll have you home before you know it.

TEENA. And then what?

VINCE. We'll get a takeaway; a bottle; you'll play us your favourite songs, I'll sing you to sleep.

TEENA. And you'll stay?

VINCE sings the last verse of 'I Got You Babe' by Sonny and Cher. After a few lines, TEENA joins in.

VINCE. I'm going nowhere.

TEENA. I love you, Vince. I love you so, so much.

VINCE. I know.

TEENA. It's not you, it's me . . . It's since my mum . . . I just can't seem to . . . I get these thoughts in me head and . . .

VINCE. It doesn't matter.

TEENA. Yes, it does. I know you'd never . . . Neil an' that . . . I know it's all in the past, I know . . .

VINCE. Ssssshhh.

TEENA. You won't leave me, will you?

VINCE. I won't leave you.

TEENA. Promise?

VINCE. Swear to Elvis. Uh-huh.

Silence.

TEENA. What are you thinking?

VINCE. What are you?

TEENA. That I don't want to go home.

VINCE. Home. (*Beat.*) A clapped-out van, clapped-out gear and a club scene that's dying on its feet.

TEENA. Is it?

VINCE. They won't want live entertainment round our way much longer. Not with quiz nights and DJs and football on the big screen.

TEENA. But what else can we do?

VINCE. Well . . . We can get on the phone and get the good gigs . . . the proper gigs . . . in London.

TEENA. London?

VINCE. That's where the money is; that's where you get discovered; that's where you start again.

TEENA. Me and you?

VINCE. Why not? We've paid our dues, we're good, we're the best we've ever been. We'll get us an audition, get a shit-hot agent, pack our bags and go.

TEENA. But what about Bernie?

VINCE. Stuff Bernie. What's he ever done but stuck us in the middle of the North Sea in November? No; from now on, there'll be no more ferries, no more bingo, no more 'turn it bloody down'. We'll do classy gigs for classy people.

TEENA. In posh hotels and stuff?

VINCE. Posh hotels, corporates, high society dos.

TEENA. I'd love to sing some jazz, and blues, and loungy stuff.

VINCE. Yeh, we'll do a bit of that and we'll charge 'em top dollar. I'm telling you, Tee: we'd clean up. I'll get my Harley, you'll get your house –

TEENA. Or one of them great big loft apartments.

VINCE. I might even come and live in it, an' all.

TEENA. Honest?

VINCE. Straight up. So what d'you think?

Beat.

TEENA. The two of us, in London.

VINCE. The three of us. You, me and the music.

The tannoy puts out an urgent Norwegian call for Satin 'n' Steel.

TEENA. Sutton and Stole. Who are they?

VINCE. The Next Big Thing. But they've got to keep singing.

TEENA. I can't, Vince. Not tonight. Not 'til I've . . .

TEENA *gestures to the urn.*

VINCE. Did she really say dump me?

TEENA. No.

VINCE. Thought not.

TEENA. Yeh, she did.

Beat.

VINCE. Shall I get you that lifeboat, then?

TEENA. Only if you're on it.

Beat.

VINCE. Tee? I wish it was the Caribbean.

TEENA. It's all right. It's my mum. She'll understand.

VINCE *takes off his jacket and puts it around* TEENA*'s shoulders.*

VINCE. This one's for her.

Scene Three

Ferry. Continuous. VINCE *returns to the stage, leaving* TEENA *on the deck.* VINCE *sings his encore song, 'Daydream Believer' by The Monkees.* TEENA *prepares to say goodbye to her mum. As* VINCE *ends the song,* TEENA *scatters the ashes. They blow away like stardust in the wind.*

Scene Four

Fire door. June 2003. Midday. VINCE *comes out to make a call on his mobile.*

VINCE. It's me.

Beat.

How are yer?

Beat.

Fine, yeh. So what have you been up to?

Beat.

How's work?

Beat.

Is it?

Beat.

Yeh, it must be.

Beat.

Ah well.

Beat.

Me? Just the usual. Just gigging and stuff. Round the clubs, mainly. Oh yeh, and up to Stalybridge, that were a good 'un. We had two hundred in, they loved it.

Beat.

She's got a name.

Beat.

She's feeling better, as it happens. Back on song.

Beat.

There's no need for that.

Beat.

Can we not talk about Teena, please?

Beat.

'Cos I've got things to do.

Beat.

Important things.

Beat.

Look, I didn't ring you up to have a row.

Beat.

Just to say . . . To let you know, I can't see you tonight.

Beat.

You won't say that when I tell you why.

Beat.

We've got an audition for Mike Norton.

Beat.

Norton.

Beat.

A top-flight agent, that's all. He phoned up yesterday. He's putting on a showcase down in London and he wants us.

Beat.

London, yeh. Top clubs, top money, top everything. He's worked with Shane Richie.

Beat.

Are you taking the piss?

Beat.

As a matter of fact, it is a big thing. It's the biggest thing that's ever happened to us.

Beat.

What's that supposed to mean?

Beat.

Well, I'm phoning you now.

Beat.

'Cos I've been busy. Things are really taking off for us, Satin 'n' Steel. So all things considered, I think it's probably best if we cool it for a while.

Beat.

Look, we've had a nice time, an't we? It's been a laugh. It's been fun. But we said from the off, that's all it was.

Beat.

I know.

Beat.

I know you have.

Beat.

I can't talk about this now.

Beat.

What are you on about?

Beat.

When did I tell you I'd leave her?

Beat.

That was a bad night. She was going through a rough patch but she's back on her feet now and –

Beat.

Well, that's my situation. You've always known that.

Beat.

I am happy.

Beat.

Tell her what?

Beat.

Are you having a laugh?

Beat.

No. No way.

Beat.

'Cos it'd finish her, that's why.

Beat.

What do you mean?

Beat.

You wouldn't dare.

Beat.

What do you think? I'd deny it.

Beat.

Don't even think about it.

Beat.

Right, I'm warning you. If I ever see you at one of our gigs –

TEENA (*off*). Vince?

VINCE. You're dead, you get me? Dead.

> VINCE *ends the call as* TEENA *comes out of the fire door carrying the sound gear.*

TEENA. It's time we weren't here.

VINCE. Right.

TEENA. Come on. People to meet, plans to make, loft apartments to view.

VINCE. Yeh.

> VINCE *puts the phone in his pocket.*

TEENA. Who was that?

VINCE. Bernie.

TEENA. Is he all right?

VINCE. Fine.

> *Beat.*

TEENA. You've not told him, have you?

VINCE. No, no.

> *Beat.*

TEENA. So what's up?

VINCE. Nowt.

TEENA. Are you nervous?

VINCE. Nah.

TEENA. Me neither. Three new songs, I can't wait.

VINCE. Let's just get down there, shall we?

TEENA. I've bought a flask of tea so we don't have to stop, and a big pack of biscuits. (*Beat.*) Vince?

VINCE. Yeh?

TEENA. Are you hungry?

VINCE. No.

TEENA *goes over and gives* VINCE *a kiss.*

TEENA. I don't believe that for a minute.

VINCE *looks at* TEENA *as if he's about to say something.*

What?

VINCE. Come on, let's rock 'n' roll.

Scene Five

Nightclub. That night. TEENA *and* VINCE *sit side by side on two high stools.*

VINCE. One, two, three, four.

They sing a slow, soulful arrangement of 'Time After Time' by Cyndi Lauper.

Scene Six

Restaurant, London. Later that night. VINCE *and* TEENA *raise a glass of champagne.*

TEENA. To us – again.

VINCE. The best club-cabaret duo this side of –

TEENA. The moon.

VINCE. The sun.

TEENA. Ur-anus.

VINCE. Steady.

TEENA. We should do 'Life on Mars', I love that.

VINCE. 'Rocket Man'.

TEENA. 'Fly Me To The Moon'.

VINCE. 'I Lost My Heart To A Starship Trooper'.

TEENA. You never told me that, Vince Steel.

VINCE. Well, you don't know everything, Teena Satin.

VINCE *takes a cigar from his jacket pocket.*

TEENA. I know we're sat in No Smoking; you'll get us chucked out.

VINCE. Not when they know who we are.

TEENA. Mike Norton's gonna ring in a minute.

VINCE. You think so?

TEENA. I know so.

VINCE. How?

TEENA. Er – did you not hear my vocal?

VINCE. Er – yeh.

TEENA. And?

Beat.

VINCE. It was all right.

TEENA. All right? It was amazinger.

VINCE. Yeh . . .

TEENA. Vince?

VINCE. What?

TEENA. It was amazinger, wasn't it?

Beat.

VINCE. It was Talent with a capital T.

TEENA. Did you see him after? He was talking to my tits.

VINCE. Was he?

TEENA. Don't look like that; like you're bothered.

VINCE. So what did he tell 'em?

TEENA. Just that he'd be in touch . . . Very, very, very, very soon. You've got your mobile?

VINCE. I've always got my mobile. You?

TEENA. I've always got my mobile.

VINCE. No more pay-as-you-go when we're living in London. We'll go straight on contract.

TEENA. I'll have to have an upgrade.

VINCE. You'll have all you ever dreamed of.

TEENA. We're gonna do it, aren't we? We're really gonna make it, you and me?

VINCE. I think perhaps, maybe, yeh . . . we are.

TEENA. No more Ren'orth Miners Welfare.

VINCE. No more Open The Box.

TEENA. No more bingo and committee men and 'don't you set up there'.

VINCE. No more sex in the van, but you can't have it all.

TEENA. We had sex in the van?

VINCE. Hartlepool.

TEENA. No, we didn't.

VINCE. Yes, we did.

TEENA. We didn't Vince.

Beat.

VINCE. Perhaps we didn't.

TEENA. It was Scunthorpe.

VINCE. Bloody hell, Tee.

TEENA. No more Scunthorpe neither. We're Park Lane and Mayfair from now on.

VINCE. We're a hotel on Vine Street.

TEENA. We're Community Chest.

VINCE. You have won second prize in a beauty contest.

TEENA. Go to jail, go directly to jail, do not pass go, do not collect two hundred pounds.

VINCE. Collect two thousand a gig.

TEENA. Two grand?!

VINCE. Easy.

TEENA. Between us?

VINCE. Each. Are we eating or what?

They look at the menus.

TEENA. Posh, in't it?

VINCE. What are moules?

TEENA. Mussels.

VINCE. I've never had mussels.

TEENA. You're telling me.

VINCE. I'm back in the gym again, come Monday.

TEENA. Here's what you're having. Club sandwich.

VINCE. Club-singer sandwich.

TEENA. Satin 'n' Steel Burger.

VINCE. One-hundred-per-cent pure talent.

TEENA. They're like an aphrodisiac – mussels.

VINCE. That's prawns.

TEENA. Do they do garlic bread?

VINCE (*clicks his fingers*). Garçon? Garlic bread for the lady.

 Beat.

TEENA. Vince? Was 'Time After Time' all right?

VINCE. Yeh.

TEENA. D'you think I picked a good 'un?

VINCE. Dover sole. Great name for an album, that.

TEENA. Did I?

VINCE. It was all right, yeh.

TEENA. It felt all right. Felt good.

VINCE. It was a nice low-key start.

TEENA. What do you mean, 'low-key'?

VINCE. Well, it gave us summat to build from.

TEENA. He liked 'Suspicious Minds'.

VINCE. Elvis, in't it? He does it every time.

TEENA. He liked you. He was watching you, I saw him.

VINCE. Teena, that's all behind me now. I'm a one-woman
 man.

TEENA. I meant he liked your voice.

 Beat.

VINCE. Yeh, I know you did. I know. But I want you to
 understand, I want you to believe me –

TEENA. I do believe you; and I don't want to talk about it. That's the past. This is the future, right?

VINCE. Right.

Beat.

TEENA. Thank you.

VINCE. For what?

TEENA. Finding me. Believing in me. Loving me.

Beat.

VINCE. Come on, what do you fancy?

TEENA. You.

VINCE. I'm for afters.

TEENA. I fancy taking this champagne to that big hotel next door and pouring it all over you.

VINCE. Garçon? Garlic bread to take out.

TEENA. I fancy whisking you off to Barbados.

VINCE. What's wrong with Bognor?

TEENA. It's hot in Barbados. The sea's dead blue. You can walk round in a thong. You can get married on the beach.

VINCE. Are we eating or what?

TEENA. Let's have a baby.

VINCE. What – for dinner?

TEENA. I'm 31. I'm getting old. Let's not leave it too late.

VINCE. Teena, we're performers.

TEENA. So? We'll take it with us. I'll get you a papoose.

VINCE. I could wear it onstage.

TEENA. Satin 'n' Steel 'n' Son. Imagine that?

VINCE. Imagine.

The mobile rings.

TEENA. Shit!

VINCE. Shit!

TEENA. Shit!

VINCE. It's all right, it's all right, I've got it.

>   VINCE *goes through his pockets to find the phone.*

TEENA. Where?

VINCE. Your bag. I put it in your bag.

>   TEENA *finds the phone in her bag and throws it to* VINCE.

VINCE. Vince Steel, Vocal Entertainer. Hello there, how you
>   doing?

TEENA. Is it him?

VINCE. Good, thanks, good. Yeh, it was. Yeh, we did. Right.
>   Right. Oh. Okay. Yeh. Mmmm. Sure. Yeh, no problem. No
>   problem at all. Yeh, I'll tell her. Yeh, Okey-dokey. We will,
>   we'll be in touch. Monday, yeh. Thank you very much.
>   Cheers. Bye.

TEENA. Well?

>   *Beat.*

VINCE. It were Bernie.

TEENA. Bloody hell, Vince. I thought it was him.

VINCE. Me too, for a minute.

TEENA. You said he didn't know about Norton.

VINCE. I know.

TEENA. You said you wouldn't say owt 'til we signed?

VINCE. I know I did but then I thought, well, you've got to
>   play fair at the end of the day. You meet 'em on the way up
>   and you meet 'em on the way down, don't yer?

TEENA. What are you on about, 'down'?

VINCE. I mean you've got to play the game, that's all. This is
>   business, in't it? Show – business.

Beat.

TEENA. So what did he say?

VINCE. Who?

TEENA. Bernie?

VINCE. Oh, he just asked how it went.

TEENA. And you told him?

VINCE. Yeh, you heard me.

TEENA. 'Yeh, right, okay.' Let me have a word.

TEENA *takes the phone, but* VINCE *takes it back.*

VINCE. Look, we've had a bit of fun so let's just calm it down. We can't get too excited 'til we know it's in the bag.

TEENA. It is.

VINCE. I know, I know, I know. So you just have another drink, right? I'm going to the bog.

TEENA. Watch out; I might follow you in.

VINCE. You just behave yourself, right? I'll be back.

VINCE *gets up to leave the table with his phone.*

TEENA. Vince?

VINCE. What?

TEENA. You can't take the call if you're having a pee. It's not professional, is it?

VINCE. No. No . . .

VINCE *puts the phone back on the table.*

TEENA. Vince?

VINCE. Now what?

TEENA. I love you.

Beat.

VINCE. Me too.

VINCE *goes to kiss her on the lips but at the last minute, kisses her on the cheek and leaves the table.* TEENA *takes a sip of champagne. She reads the menu again, then puts it down. She looks around self-consciously. Her eyes are drawn back to the mobile phone. She has another drink, looks around, but curiosity gets the better of her. She picks up the mobile, presses a few keys and reads the display as* VINCE *returns.*

TEENA. That were quick.

VINCE. I couldn't find it.

TEENA. Ask the waiter.

VINCE. I'm all right.

> TEENA *toys with the mobile.*

TEENA. So what else did Bernie say?

VINCE. Not much.

TEENA. Come on, what did he ask you?

VINCE. Nowt.

TEENA. What did he tell you to tell me?

> *Beat.*

VINCE. Just that we're gigging on Wednesday.

TEENA. I can't do Wednesday.

VINCE. 'Course you can.

TEENA. I can't. I'll ring him in a minute and tell him.

VINCE. You know what, Tee? I think we should get off. It's silly money, this. I think we should go, luv. I mean, it's thirty quid to park the van.

TEENA. Great, aren't they? Mobile phones.

VINCE. Yeh, they're brilliant, come on.

TEENA. You know what I like best about 'em? This. 'Received calls.'

VINCE. Teena, give it here.

VINCE tries to grab the phone but TEENA *pulls away.*

TEENA. Hello, is that Bernard Matthews? It's not. Oh, sorry about that, who is it, then? . . . Oh . . . Yes, hello, it's Teena Satin here. You've just spoke to Vince . . . That's right, yes . . . No, he didn't tell me, no . . . Yes, please. (*Silence.*) Right. Okay. Right. Right. Okay. (*Silence.*) No, I would. I am. Thank you . . . Bye. Bye.

Silence.

VINCE. I'll get the bill, shall I?

Silence.

I was gonna tell you.

Silence.

He doesn't want us, Teena.

TEENA. No.

VINCE. So that's that, then, come on –

TEENA. He wants me.

VINCE. 'Course he does, he was eyeing up your tits.

TEENA. Mike Norton wants me.

VINCE. Well, tough. We're a duo.

TEENA. He wants me.

VINCE. We're a duo.

TEENA. You're a liar.

VINCE. So stuff Norton and stuff London. We can do it on us own.

TEENA. You're a liar.

VINCE. I found you, I made you. Christ, you couldn't have sung that song before me.

TEENA. You're a liar.

Beat.

VINCE. All right, all right, I am, I know I am, I know . . . but
I'm not strong like you, I'm weak . . . I'm weak . . . I'm
weak and a bastard and a liar but there's something inside
me that I just can't . . . I know . . . But there's one good
thing about me, and that's you. You. 'Cos we're meant for
each other, me and you. We're amazinger, we're *je ne sais
quoi.* We're Satin 'n' Steel . . . We're Satin 'n' Steel . . . and
I can change. I can change. I won't lie, I'll never lie to you
again. I'll get the good gigs, I'll take you to Barbados
and I'll marry you, I'll marry you, that's what I'll do and
I promise you, I promise you I'll stand by my vows, I'll be
faithful and true and don't look at me like that . . . Teena . . .
I'm telling you the truth . . . I am . . . And . . . And all right,
all right, there has been someone else . . . there was . . . but
it's not Neil, I promise you it's not . . . He just lives up the
road . . . He's just a kid, well, not a kid, he's 22 but it's just
a bit of fun and he means nothing to me, nothing . . . See,
I'm telling you the truth . . . It's all out in the open . . . and
it's over now, it's totally finished . . . I told him today,
I dumped him for you; 'cos it's you I want; it's you; and
I promise you, I promise you faithfully, this time, I'll stop.
I'll never do it again. Never. Teena, please, I know I'm bad,
but you, you're good and you can help me, you can save
me, you can . . . We'll get married, move away and . . .
Teena, please? Please . . . I love you. I love you. I need you.
I want you.

TEENA. And you've had me.

Now go.

VINCE *waits. She says nothing.* VINCE *leaves.*

Scene Seven

Miners' Welfare Club. November 2004. As VINCE *is packing up the gear,* TEENA *comes back in.*

TEENA. Vince?

VINCE. Yeh?

TEENA. My keys. I left my car keys.

VINCE. Oh. Right.

VINCE *finds* TEENA*'s keys on the amp.*

You're driving now?

TEENA. I'm learning. Clive's got me a car. Just a Yugo, you know, but he's doing it up.

VINCE. A Yugo?

TEENA. A sporty one.

VINCE. What colour is it?

TEENA. Red, Michael.

VINCE. He's looking after you, then?

TEENA. Well . . . It's early days, but yeh.

Beat.

VINCE. I know nowt about cars.

TEENA. Or vans.

VINCE. I scrapped it in the end. I dunno know how it kept going all them years.

TEENA. It ran on love as I remember.

Beat.

VINCE. Teena –

TEENA. My keys.

VINCE *gives her the keys.*

VINCE. Mirror – signal – manoeuvre.

TEENA. Yeh.

VINCE. Take it steady. Watch your speed.

TEENA. I will.

VINCE. And you know where to find us if you're passing.

Beat.

TEENA. I didn't come here for a fight or owt. I just wanted to tell you to your face.

VINCE. Tell me what?

TEENA. That I know what you are and what you want; and I was wrong to try and change you.

VINCE. But you did change me.

TEENA. Did I?

VINCE. That night here, remember; when I first saw you sing? Tee, you blew me away.

TEENA. Yeh, well, I'd best get back.

VINCE. I'd best get on.

Beat.

TEENA. Have a good 'un. Break a leg.

VINCE. Ta.

Beat.

TEENA. I'll see you then, Vince.

VINCE. Yeh, see you.

TEENA *turns to go.*

So how was it?

TEENA. What?

VINCE. London. Were you gigging or what?

TEENA. Yeh. (*Beat.*) Mike did what he said. Got me the gear, got me out there. I did all the hotels, the corporates, that kind of thing. Got a room in Penge. It were all right; it were good.

VINCE. Good.

TEENA. Mike was managing this young lass and I did some work for her. Backing vocals mainly; in the studio.

VINCE. Which one?

TEENA. Can't remember. He got the girl a deal though; she worked hard for it, an' all. She had a personal trainer and everything.

VINCE. Can she sing though?

TEENA. She can hold a tune. And you should see what they can do in the studio these days. All them computers; all them knobs.

VINCE. Like Mike.

TEENA. He's not that bad.

VINCE. Did he shag you?

TEENA. No Vince, he didn't shag me.

VINCE. I bet he had a go though?

TEENA. 'Course he did.

VINCE. Is that why you came back?

TEENA. No. (*Beat.*) Look, it's time I wasn't here –

VINCE. Tee? Tell us.

Beat.

TEENA. I came back 'cos I didn't like the Tube.

VINCE. Right.

TEENA. Or the traffic; or turning up to gigs on my own.
I don't mind hard work but it were different down there.
I was the wrong side of town, the wrong side of thirty . . .

You need more than a voice, you need . . . Well, whatever it was, I've not got it, so . . .

VINCE. Will you do us a favour?

TEENA. What?

VINCE. I want to hear what it sounds like from the back.

TEENA. Vince –

VINCE. Just for a level. Please. Come on.

TEENA *takes the microphone.* VINCE *goes to the back of the hall.*

TEENA (*into the microphone*). Macaroni, macaroni.

VINCE. I can't get it from that.

TEENA. La-la-la-la-la-la-la-la.

VINCE. Now with music.

TEENA. No.

VINCE. How else can I hear it?

TEENA *turns on the sound. The song is 'Wind Beneath My Wings' by Bette Midler.*

TEENA. Vince, I can't.

VINCE. Just a couple of bars.

TEENA *sings the opening lines.*

TEENA. Is that enough?

VINCE. A bit more, luv.

TEENA *sings a little more, very reluctantly.*

TEENA. It sounds fine.

VINCE. I just need to hear the loud bit.

TEENA *sings the verse and goes into the chorus. She's never sounded better. As she ends the first chorus,* VINCE *returns to the stage and turns the backing track off, cutting her off mid-song.*

VINCE. That's it.

TEENA. Looks like the gear's all right.

VINCE. Just takes a bit of warming up.

TEENA. Don't we all?

Beat.

VINCE. I'd better do my hair, then. You'd best get off.

TEENA. Spray it up. You'll be surprised how you sweat.

VINCE. Go on. Don't wanna keep the old folks waiting.

TEENA. Vince –

VINCE. Watch them roads.

TEENA. How's it going, you know . . . With him – boy wonder?

Beat.

VINCE. He's not a boy, he's 23.

TEENA. How's it going?

VINCE. Oh . . . It's not.

TEENA. I heard you'd moved him in?

VINCE. I did for a bit but . . . Well, I'm not so easy to live with, am I? Being an entertainer an' all that.

Beat.

TEENA. I'm sorry.

VINCE. Don't be. It's not your fault, is it?

Beat.

TEENA. I gave it everything, you know? Satin 'n' Steel.

VINCE. I know you did.

TEENA. Perhaps it just weren't meant to be?

VINCE. All they want today is kids with click tracks. They wouldn't know a singer if it hit 'em in the face.

TEENA. But we had it once, didn't we? You and me?

Beat.

VINCE. We had it.

Beat.

TEENA. Thank you, Vince.

Beat.

VINCE. Go on, then. You've got a fella out there waiting.

TEENA. Well . . . It's a whole new beginning, is this.

VINCE. New Beginning. Now there's a name to conjure with.

TEENA. You're solo. Why not use your real name?

VINCE. This is showbiz, Teena Satin. The stuff of which
dreams are made.

TEENA gives VINCE a goodbye kiss.

TEENA. I hope you make it, Vince.

VINCE. I will. 'Course I will.

*TEENA leaves the club. VINCE watches her go without a
word.*

*Alone again, he looks around the club and speaks into
microphone.*

Than'youverymuch.

Beat.

Goodnight.

Slow fade to black.

The End.

A Nick Hern Book

Satin 'n' Steel first published in Great Britain as a paperback original in 2005 by Nick Hern Books Limited, 14 Larden Road, London W3 7ST, in association with Nottingham Playhouse

Satin 'n' Steel copyright © 2005 Amanda Whittington

Amanda Whittington has asserted her right to be identified as the author of this work

Cover image: Norman Pace and Sara Poyzer as Satin 'n' Steel. Photography by Robert Day

Typeset by Country Setting, Kingsdown, Kent CT14 8ES
Printed and bound in Great Britain by Bookmarque, Croydon, Surrey

A CIP catalogue record for this book is available from the British Library

ISBN 1 85459 865 1

CAUTION All rights whatsoever in this play are strictly reserved. Requests to reproduce the text in whole or in part should be addressed to the publisher.

Amateur Performing Rights Applications for performance, including readings and excerpts, by amateurs (and by stock companies in the United States of America and Canada) should be addressed to the Performing Rights Manager, Nick Hern Books, 14 Larden Road, London W3 7ST, *fax* +44 (0)20 8735 0250, *e-mail* info@nickhernbooks.demon.co.uk, except as follows:

Australia:Dominie Drama, 8 Cross Street, Brookvale 2100, *fax* (2) 9905 5209, *e-mail* dominie@dominie.com.au

New Zealand: Play Bureau, PO Box 420, New Plymouth, *fax* (6)753 2150, *e-mail* play.bureau.nz@xtra.co.nz

Professional Performing Rights Applications for performance by professionals in any medium and in any language throughout the world (except by stock companies in North America: see above) should be addressed to MBA Literary Agents Ltd, 62 Grafton Way, London W1T 5DW, *fax* +44 (0)20 7327 2042, *e-mail* meg@mbalit.co.uk

No performance of any kind may be given unless a licence has been obtained. Applications should be made before rehearsals begin. Publication of this play does not necessarily indicate its availability for performance.

Other Titles in this Series

Patrick Barlow
LOVE UPON THE THRONE
THE MESSIAH
THE WONDER OF SEX

Laurence Boswell
BEAUTY AND THE BEAST

Caryl Churchill
BLUE HEART
CHURCHILL PLAYS: THREE
CHURCHILL: SHORTS
CLOUD NINE
A DREAM PLAY *after* Strindberg
FAR AWAY
HOTEL
ICECREAM
LIGHT SHINING IN
    BUCKINGHAMSHIRE
MAD FOREST
A NUMBER
THE SKRIKER
THIS IS A CHAIR
THYESTES *after* Seneca
TRAPS

Dominic Cooke
ARABIAN NIGHTS

Helen Cooper
THREE WOMEN AND
    A PIANO TUNER

Helen Edmundson
ANNA KARENINA *after* Tolstoy
THE CLEARING
GONE TO EARTH *after* Webb
THE MILL ON THE FLOSS
    after Eliot
MOTHER TERESA IS DEAD
WAR AND PEACE *after* Tolstoy

Heimann / Monaghan / Petterle
100

Liz Lochhead
MEDEA *after* Euripides
MISERY GUTS *after* Molière
PERFECT DAYS
THEBANS *after* Euripides and
Sophocles

Tim Luscombe
NORTHANGER ABBEY
    after Austen

Clare McIntyre
THE MATHS TUTOR
MY HEART'S A SUITCASE
    & LOW LEVEL PANIC
THE THICKNESS OF SKIN

Conor McPherson
DUBLIN CAROL
McPHERSON: FOUR PLAYS
McPHERSON PLAYS: TWO
PORT AUTHORITY
SHINING CITY
THE WEIR

Martin Millar & Doon MacKichan
EMMA *after* Austen

Arthur Miller
AN ENEMY OF THE PEOPLE
    after Ibsen
PLAYING FOR TIME

Stuart Paterson
CINDERELLA
HANSEL AND GRETEL

Diane Samuels
KINDERTRANSPORT
THE TRUE LIFE FICTION
    OF MATA HARI

Imogen Stubbs
WE HAPPY FEW

Polly Teale
AFTER MRS ROCHESTER
JANE EYRE *after* Brontë

Lawrence Till
KES *after* Barry Hines

Paul Webb
FOUR NIGHTS IN
    KNARESBOROUGH

Fay Weldon
MADAME BOVARY *after* Flaubert

Amanda Whittington
BE MY BABY

Ian Wooldridge
ANIMAL FARM *after* Orwell

Nicholas Wright
CRESSIDA
HIS DARK MATERIALS
    after Pullman
MRS KLEIN
VINCENT IN BRIXTON
WRIGHT: FIVE PLAYS